Gulf Islands N

POCK

Randi Minetor

Photographs by Nic Minetor

FALCONGUIDES ®

GUILFORD, CONNECTICUT
HELENA, MONTANA

AN IMPRINT OF THE GLOBE PEQUOT PRESS

FACT SHEET

Established: January 8, 1971

Time zone: Central Time

Park hours: Open year-round, with seasonal hours in some areas. West Ship Island is open 7:00 a.m. to sunset daily; all other Mississippi islands are open twenty-four hours. Davis Bayou is open 6:00 a.m. to sunset daily. In Florida, the Okaloosa Area is open 7:00 a.m. to sunset, Santa Rosa and Perdido Key are open 8:00 a.m. to sunset.

Size: 160 miles long; 80 percent of the park is submerged land in the Gulf of Mexico.

Visitation: 2,034,294 visits in 2007.

Elevation: Sea level to 30 feet; the high elevation varies with the dune's height.

Beaches: Three named beaches in Florida: Langdon, Opal, and Rosamond Johnson Beach. West Ship Island is in the Mississippi District.

Islands: Six barrier islands: Santa Rosa Island and Perdido Key in Florida, and Petit Bois, Horn, and East and West Ship islands in Mississippi, as well as a portion of Cat Island

Forts: Four: Fort Barrancas, Advanced Redoubt, and Fort Pickens in Florida, and Fort Massachusetts in Mississippi

Visitor centers: Four: Naval Live Oaks, Fort Barrancas, William M. Colmer Visitor Center (Davis Bayou), and Fort Pickens

Campgrounds: There are 35 miles of trails in the Florida district, and 2 miles in the Mississippi district. Two front-country campgrounds: Fort Pickens and Davis Bayou; backcountry beach camping is permitted in some areas.

Animal species count: 280 bird species, 24 mammal species, 14 amphibian species, and 47 reptile species, including 18 species of snakes

Park information: (850) 934-2600 in Florida, (228) 875-9057, ext. 100 in Mississippi

Park Web site: www.nps .gov/guis

Contents

Welcome:
Introduction to Gulf Islands National Seashore

On the southern coast of the Florida Panhandle, stretching eastward to the tip of Mississippi, lies a 160-mile expanse of blindingly white beaches, intensely blue-green water, and windswept barrier islands—the survivors of thousands of years of shifting dunes, tropical storms, and the changing hands of human conflict and settlement.

This ribbon of sparkling sand and water is Gulf Islands National Seashore, and it provides a recreational experience like no other coastline retreat in the continental United States. A short walk brings miles of uninterrupted, sugar-white sand within easy reach, giving visitors access to a peaceful solitude they may not expect to find on the otherwise-congested Florida coastline. Islands several miles off the Mississippi shore remain undeveloped oases of sand held

◀ *Dunes help protect the mainland from frequent storms.*

together by the roots and stems of sea oats, a tenacious plant with a critically important role in the islands' life cycle. On the mainland, bayous bring fresh- and salt water together to create a haven for plants, birds, animals, and fish that require this balanced mix to thrive, while tranquil vistas of nodding vegetation extend before us—a home for chattering kingfishers, bobbing grebes and ducks, the occasional leap of a playful dolphin, and slow-moving, sun-dappled waters.

Preserved as a unit of the National Park Service since 1971, Gulf Islands National Seashore battles annually for its life against a barrage of hurricane gales and storm surges that threaten to consume its islands and shores. Extensive damage from hurricanes Ivan and Dennis in 2004 and 2005 destroyed the roads to Fort Pickens to the west and Navarre Beach to the east. Both of these roads are expected to reopen in 2009, but the coastline between Pensacola Beach and Fort Pickens is 30 yards narrower than it was in 2004. The remaining beach still provides an unbroken, 7-mile length of white sand for visitors to enjoy, but it stands as a dramatic example of the change that natural forces can wreak overnight.

Indeed, the beach and coastline you see today could extend farther out into the sea on your next visit, or your view could be blocked by newly formed dunes as windblown sand settles into sculpted formations . . . or one island could be split into two by a storm-dredged canal. The fascination of this seashore is its state of constant change, a natural process the park has taken significant steps to preserve.

As these islands and coastlines change, however, they serve to protect the mainland by absorbing the first impact of hurricane winds, creating natural drainage systems that dispatch floodwaters back into the gulf, and re-forming over centuries to provide new barriers against storm surges. This seashore plays a critical role in keeping the areas farther inland comparatively undisturbed by gale winds, making its survival an important contributor to the quality of life for th Florida panhandle and the Mississippi Gulf Coast.

Beyond its natural significance, Gulf Islands has seen a generous slice of

Fort Pickens is one of four historic forts in the park. ▶

early colonization and military history. Archaeologists have found evidence of Paleo-Indian villages on the beaches, indicating the existence of human life here as much as 5,000 years ago. Spanish settlers in the 1700s built batteries on land now included in the national seashore, defending themselves against invasion by other European colonial powers. In the 1800s, the United States government saw the strategic value of this land along the northern Gulf Coast and its vulnerability to attack, ordering the construction of five brick forts (four of which remain) as part of the nation's Third System of coastal defense. Today, visitors can tour these impressive structures and imagine their preparation for an invasion that did not come until the Civil War.

Whether your interest lies in miles of gleaming white beach and turquoise water, in American military history, or in the abundant foliage and wildlife that make these shores their home, you will find a wealth of opportunities for outdoor exploration, wilderness adventure, and lessons about our nation's earliest years in the Gulf Islands. Explore on foot, on a bicycle, in your car, or by boat, and find your way to the edge of the continent, where freshwater meets salt and land meets sea . . . and where visitors discover what a treasure an untouched, undeveloped seashore can be.

◀ *Sugar-white sand and emerald water are the hallmarks of the Gulf Islands.*

Navigate:
Getting to and around the Park

Gulf Islands National Seashore is south of Interstate 10 in both Mississippi and Florida.

By air: Fly into Pensacola Gulf Coast Regional Airport in Florida or the Gulfport-Biloxi International Airport in Mississippi.

By bus: Greyhound Bus Line serves Pensacola, Gulfport, and Biloxi.

By boat: Some of the Gulf Islands are accessible only by passenger ferry or chartered boat. The ferry service Ship Island Excursions at US 90 and US 49 in Gulfport, Mississippi, is the official boat transportation company for East and West Ship Islands; the ferry runs from March through October. Call 866-GO-MS-FUN or visit www .msshipisland.com for current schedules and rates.

By car: To Mississippi park headquarters, from the west, take

◀ *Many major roads lead to the seashore.*

I-10 to exit 50. From this exit, travel south on Mississippi Highway 609 to U.S. Highway 90, and turn left (east) onto US 90. Continue to Park Road; turn right and follow this road to the visitor center. From the east, take exit 57 south, then turn right on US 90, and continue to the park entrance (on the left). **To Florida park headquarters,** from I-10, take exit 12 (Interstate 110) and drive south on I-110 to its end at U.S. Highway 98. Take US 98 south across Pensacola Bay and into Gulf Breeze, and continue on US 98 to Naval Live Oaks.

Park Fees and Entrances

General admission: Entrance fees are charged at Fort Pickens, Perdido Key, and seasonally at Opal Beach: $8 per vehicle or $3 per individual (or motorcycle or bicycle rider), good for seven days. Purchase an annual pass for $25. A Night Owl Pass for $30 provides after-hours access to the fee-area beaches and islands.

Activity fees: There is a $16 fee per night at Davis Bayou Campground. Camping at Fort Pickens Campground is $20 per night. The Davis Bayou Boat Launch is $3 per day; an annual pass is $20.

Park entrances: In Florida, there are several ways to enter the park. Visit the Naval Live Oaks area on US 98 in Gulf Breeze, or continue over the bridge to Pensacola Beach and enter the park's beach areas by driving to the end of either Fort Pickens Road (to the west) or Via De Luna Drive to

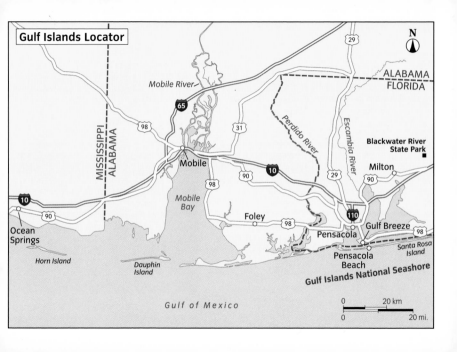

J. Earle Bowden Way (to the east). You can reach another pristine beach by driving through Pensacola and then taking Florida Highway 292 west to Rosamond Johnson Beach at the Perdido Key area, which is across Pensacola Bay.

The Davis Bayou area is the only mainland unit of the park in Mississippi, and it is easily reached from US 90 in the middle of Ocean Springs. To visit West Ship Island in Mississippi Sound, take the ferry boat from Gulfport, Mississippi (see "By boat," above). A visit to the wilderness islands requires a licensed National Park Service boat captain; for more information, visit www.nps.gov/guis/planyourvisit/transportation-to-wilderness-islands.htm.

Visitor Centers

William M. Colmer Visitor Center in Davis Bayou is open daily, 8:30 a.m. to 4:30 p.m., (228) 875-9057, ext. 100. The visitor center features interpretive displays about the bayou ecosystem and the plants, animals, marine life, and birds that make it their home.

The dock at Colmer Visitor Center provides pleasant walks along Mississippi Sound.

Naval Live Oaks Visitor Center is open daily from 8:30 a.m. to 4:30 p.m.; it is closed on Christmas Day. New exhibits tell the story of the live oaks—oak trees that appear ever-green throughout the year—and their significance to shipbuilding. Volunteers and rangers can help you identify the unusual plants and birds you may see on the nearby Brackenridge Nature Trail, and it's a short walk to the Santa Rosa Sound shore.

Fort Barrancas Visitor Center (850-455-5167) keeps seasonal hours: March through October, 9:30 a.m. to 4:45 p.m.; November through February, 8:30 a.m. to 3:45 p.m. Tours of the fort are given daily. To visit, you will drive onto the Pensacola Naval Air Station, a working base for the U.S. Navy.

Fort Barrancas Visitor Center is on Pensacola Naval Air Station.

Stop at the security checkpoint at the base entrance, where you will receive a pass that allows you to visit Fort Barrancas, Pensacola Lighthouse, and the National Naval Aviation Museum. To enter the base, you must have a valid driver's license or picture ID, proof of valid auto insurance, and a current state vehicle registration. Bicycle and motorcycle riders must wear helmets. Note that personal weapons of any kind are not permitted on any U.S. military base, and visitors on base cannot use mobile phones while operating a vehicle.

Fort Pickens Visitor Center, an information station and bookstore adjacent to the fort, is open for self-guided tours from 8:00 a.m. to sunset daily. Guided tours are given daily at 2:00 p.m.

Visitor Services

ATM and gas: On Pensacola Beach, Surfside Food & Store is at 22 Via De Luna Drive, (850) 934-4576. You'll find plenty of gas stations along Florida Highway 30 as you approach the park. In Ocean Springs, there's a Shell station at 2875 Bienville Boulevard, (228) 875-2584, and an Exxon at 3074 Government Street, (228) 875-2035.

Film and camera supplies: On Pensacola Beach, you'll find Camera Technologies, 3 Casino Beach Boardwalk, (850) 934-4875. Try the Rite Aid at 3164 Bienville Road in Ocean Springs for film and disposable cameras.

Gift shops: All park visitor centers have bookstores managed by Eastern National, featuring books, logo items, and gifts. Souvenirs are available from the concessionaires at Fort Pickens and at the boat dock on West Ship Island.

Internet service: Peg Leg Pete's, 1010 Fort Pickens Road on Pensacola Beach, offers free Wi-Fi. Coffee Fusion t 2228 Bienville Boulevard in Ocean Springs is a free Wi-Fi hot spot. (Coffee Fusion also serves some yummy bubble tea.)

Laundry: Beach Laundry, 37 Via De Luna Drive on Pensacola Beach, (850) 932-3005. In Ocean Springs, Coastal Coin Laundry is at 2406 Government Street, (228) 872-4758.

Lost and found: (850) 934-2600 in Florida, (228) 875-9057, ext. 100 in Mississippi

Medical: In an emergency, dial 911. In Florida, the closest medical center is Gulf Breeze Hospital, 1110 Gulf Breeze Parkway, (850) 934-2000. In Mississippi, Ocean Springs Hospital is close to the park at 3109 Bienville Boulevard (US 90), (228) 818-1111.

Pharmacy: CVS pharmacies can be found at 225, 713, and 3327 Gulf Breeze Parkway (FL 30) in Gulf Breeze. You'll find a Rite Aid pharmacy at 3082 Bienville Boulevard in Ocean Springs, and a CVS at 2190 Bienville Boulevard.

Post office: 100 Northcliff Drive in Gulf Breeze; 1581 Bienville Boulevard in Ocean Springs.

Religious services: Pensacola Beach Community Church, 916 Panferio Drive in Gulf Breeze, (850) 932-6628; Unity of Gulf Breeze, 913 Gulf Breeze Parkway #26, (850) 932-3076. In Ocean Springs, the closest churches are Grace Church Gulf Coast, 14 Marks Road, (228) 818-2989, and Christus Victor Lutheran Church, 2755 Bienville Boulevard, (228) 875-2446. There are many other churches; check local listings.

Showers: Showers are available at the Fort Pickens campground in Florida, and at the Davis Bayou campground in Mississippi.

Stores and supplies: There's a Publix Super Market at 852 Gulf Breeze Parkway, just over the bridge in Gulf Breeze. In Ocean Springs, Rouses Market is adjacent to the park entrance at 3164 Bienville Boulevard, (228) 875-1687. Winn-Dixie is at 1515 Bienville Boulevard, (228) 875-8388.

Park Rules, Regulations, and Safety Tips

Alcohol: Open containers are not permitted in vehicles. Glass containers are prohibited on the Mississippi islands and on the Florida beaches.

Backcountry camping: Primitive camping is allowed on Perdido Key (with a free permit from the ranger's office) and on Horn, Petit Bois, East Ship, and the public section of Cat Island. There are no camping facilities on the islands, and you will need your own boat transportation to get to them (visit www.nps.gov/guis/planyourvisit/transportation-to-wilderness-islands.htm for a list of approved charter boat operators).

Beach safety: Watch for beach-safety warning flags at all lifeguard-protected beaches. Swim at lifeguard-protected beaches (seasonally)—Johnson, Langdon, Opal, and West Ship Island—and never swim alone. Sandbars are often shallow; remember "feet first, first time." Rip currents are real and can be dangerous; know what to do if you are caught in one.

Boating: Safe boating requires a craft of 20 feet or longer to handle the open water. Inland water boats (like pontoon or bass boats) are not appropriate for boating to the islands. Bring an updated nautical chart with the most current information about shoals and obstructions, and leave a float plan with a family member or friend. Be aware of tides, and be ready to move your boat if the weather changes.

Firearms: At the very least, firearms may be transported in all areas of the park (except Fort Barrancas, because it is located within a military base) in vehicles if they are unloaded and

Flag colors let you know when it's safe to swim.

stowed in a manner so that they are not immediately accessible to occupants. A new regulation may soon go into effect that may be more permissible. Regulations concerning the carry and transport of firearms in the park are complicated and subject to change. Contact park staff for details in advance of your trip. Fireworks are not allowed in the park.

Fires: Fires are allowed on the beach camping area (½ mile east of the end of the road) below the high-tide line at the Perdido Key area and on all the Mississippi islands but West Ship. Do not build fires in wooded areas or on the dunes.

Fishing: You must have a Mississippi saltwater sportfishing license to fish in

You don't need a license to fish from a Florida fishing pier.

the park in Mississippi. If you are fishing for recreation from the Fort Pickens pier, you do not need a license, but all other Florida fishing requires a state fishing license. Get your Florida license at www.MyFWC.com. In Mississippi, call 1-800-5GO-HUNT or visit home. mdwfp.com/Default.aspx.

Food: No glass bottles or containers are permitted on Mississippi islands or park beaches. While picnics are encouraged, please do not feed wildlife or leave food scraps that may attract birds and other animals.

Insects: Mosquitoes and gnats are active in the winter and spring, especially at dawn and dusk. Use a good insect repellent when hiking on trails. Watch for ants inside Fort Pickens, and biting fire ants in many places throughout the national seashore.

Personal watercraft: Gulf Islands National Seashore permits the use of personal watercraft in some areas of the park. For a detailed list, visit www.nps.gov/guis/parkmgmt/personal-watercraft.htm.

Pets: Pets are not allowed on Florida beaches, on the beach at West Ship Island, or on Horn or Petit Bois wilderness islands. Walk your pet on trails or on the park roads, but keep your pet on a leash no longer than 6 feet. Pets are not allowed in pavilions or forts. Service animals are allowed. You are required to clean up after your pet.

Sharks and stingrays: To avoid the possibility of contact with a shark, do not swim at dawn, dusk, or at night when sharks are feeding. Stay away from murky waters. Do the "stingray shuffle": shuffle your feet in the sand underwater to avoid stepping on stingrays. If you are injured by a stingray, soak the affected area in extremely hot water to alleviate the pain, and then seek medical attention.

Jellyfish: Ask the lifeguard if jellyfish are present. If stung, apply vinegar to the affected area. Do not wash with freshwater or touch the irritated skin.

Snakes: The seashore is home to several species of venomous snakes, which can appear on trails, on the islands, and in the bayou. Give snakes their space and watch them from a distance. If you encounter one suddenly at close range, don't try to touch or catch it—just leave it alone and walk away. Snakes are not aggressive, and most will flee when approached by people. All wildlife within the park is protected by federal law.

Speed limits: Posted speed limits vary throughout the seashore. Please obey all speed limits.

Trash: Deposit all trash in receptacles that are provided by the park. Many areas including Santa Rosa, West Ship Island, and the wilderness islands are "pack it in, pack it out" areas, so please take all of your trash with you when you leave.

Wildlife: Feeding wildlife is prohibited, and those caught feeding birds and animals or harassing alligators are subject to fines of up to $5,000. Please enjoy the park's wildlife from a distance.

Weather in the Park

Temperate winters and hot, breezy summers are the norm in the Florida and Mississippi panhandles, with winter highs in the 60s from December through March, dipping down into the 40s at night. Spring and fall can be spectacular here, with bright, sunny days that hover in the 70s and low 80s, and clear evenings in the 50s and 60s. Summers bring the wet season, with alternating blue skies and short, intermittent rains, often from thunderstorms. Temperatures in June, July, August, and early September average in the 90s by day and the 70s at night.

Hurricane season is June 1 through November 30, and these tropical storms are serious business. Park areas close when a storm is expected. The Fort Pickens area may also experience temporary closures throughout the year when storm surges cause the Fort Pickens Road to flood. If you are planning a major coastline hike or a boat

Blue skies and bright sun reveal hurricanes' impact on Gulf beaches.

trip during hurricane season, be sure to check with the park's visitor centers or with the National Weather Service before venturing out on your own.

History.

Key Things about the Park

Chockablock with drama, struggle, triumph, and strife, the history of Gulf Islands National Seashore is a tale of misguided explorations, violent storms, valor in the face of adversity, desperation and tenacity . . . and, finally, a narrow strip of unblemished beach and a seacoast dotted with wind-whipped islands.

White Sands from Mountaintops

It's quartz! The sparkling white sand that stops visitors in their tracks when they first glimpse the Gulf Islands beach actually arrived here thousands of years ago, courtesy of rivers that washed quartz-laden silt down from the Appalachian Mountains. Probably swollen by glacial melt, the rivers brought the mineral to the open sea, where littoral currents (flowing parallel to the

◀ *The Water Battery remains from the days when Spain held Pensacola.*

Beach maintenance projects can create these snowlike dunes.

shoreline) carried the sand westward along the coast.

The current then pushed the sand back against the shore, eventually forming a ridgeline in the shallow waters. Over time, the islands' peaks rose above the water, where wind-blown seeds from mainland plants could germinate and grow, their roots establishing the cohesion that holds these fragile islands together. Today this natural process continues, forming and un-forming islands and dunes over the course of centuries or millennia—or, sometimes, in a single afternoon.

From Indians to Spanish Explorers

We know that American Indians found their way to the islands long before European settlement, but little else about their way of life. Arrowheads found on Horn and Ship Islands tell us that Indians probably hunted here, and evidence of middens hints that they settled and stayed, placing this early human habitation in the continent's timeline between 6000 and 2000 B.C.

Later, two specific tribes built villages along the coastline. The Panzacola Indians made their homes along the coast, but traveled regularly to collect food from wooded areas. Over time, many of these people moved farther inland to good farmland and natural food sources, but some remained on the coastline, and it was this group of Indians who met the first Spanish explorers in the early 1500s.

In 1559, braving a series of tropical storms in the middle of August, Don Tristán de Luna y Arellano—the man selected by Spain's King Philip II to become the governor of Florida—made landfall somewhere in Pensacola Bay. Tormented by more hurricanes, illness, and death, de Luna's colony could not survive.

Nonetheless, Pensacola celebrated 2009 as its 450th anniversary year, based on de Luna's attempt to build a settlement here; failed or not, this was the first European colony in the New World, six years before St. Augustine, Florida (which thrived), and nearly fifty years before Jamestown, which was established in 1607. Today, a cross stands on a remnant dune on Pensacola Beach, near the entrance to the seashore's Fort Pickens unit, commemorating the first Christian service in Florida.

This cross commemorates the first Christian service in Florida in 1559.

Hurricanes Can't Keep Colonists Down

Nearly 125 years would pass before settlers of any European nationality would take an interest in this corner of the New World again. In the late 1600s, both England and France began to consider the northern Gulf Coast as a potentially important area, re-piquing Spain's interest as well. Spain sent no less than eleven exploratory missions to the Florida coast, establishing a settlement near the present Fort Barrancas in 1698, but the French moved westward, focusing their attention on the Mississippi Delta under the leadership of Pierre Le Moyne d'Iberville, who used Ship Island as his base while protecting the new colony from potential Spanish invasion.

Over the next hundred years, the Spanish worked to defend and settle the Islands near Pensacola, but the repeated challenges they encountered in attempting to settle the area would finally lead Spain to cede the land to the United States in 1821. The area's strategic position on the Gulf Coast made it the logical place to build a major navy yard, but this was not the only consideration in the U.S. government's interest: The Florida panhandle contained hundreds of thousands of acres of live oaks, a durable, disease-resistant wood particularly well suited to shipbuilding. In 1828, by order of President John Quincy Adams, the U.S. Navy authorized the purchase of land to create the first United States tree farm, eventually preserving more than 60,000 acres.

The U. S. government was eager to keep its new possession safe and to protect its resources. To date, the government had a First System of forts in place—those inherited from the British ownership of the New World—and a Second System, built in a hurried attempt to create a defensive perimeter around the new country. When the British captured Washington, D.C., and burned the Capitol Building in 1814, the government recognized the inadequacy of its coastal defenses. As a further illustration, 10,000 British soldiers used Ship Island in Mississippi Sound as a rendezvous point before attacking New Orleans in the last battle of the War of 1812.

Live oaks were the building material of choice for naval ships.

The walls of Fort Pickens are several feet thick.

Construction began on a Third System of fortifications along the U.S. coast. Many of these forts involve tall, several-feet-thick brick walls shielding big guns. Fort Pickens, the largest fort in the Gulf Islands, was completed in 1834 and stood ready to protect the coast until 1947. Fort McRee stood opposite Fort Pickens on Perdido Key for many years, but did not survive the Civil War, and its ruins eventually disappeared with the tropical storms.

Fort Barrancas, built over the ruins of the Spanish fort that preceded it, took five years to construct and was completed in 1844. The nearby Advanced Redoubt was added specifically to defend the Pensacola Navy Yard. Finally, construction started in 1859 on Fort Massachusetts, built on what is now West Ship Island. Construction of seacoast forts was halted in 1870, however, and neither Fort Massachusetts nor Advanced Redoubt ever saw completion.

Twentieth-century Gulf Islands

With the Civil War finally over and its forts and live oaks made obsolete by new combat methods, the U.S. military announced plans to construct a naval air station in Pensacola, in preparation for the use of new aviation technology. Throughout World War I and then again in World War II, Pensacola became a center of military activity, both at the new naval air station and at its historic forts. Fort Barrancas's army post served as the headquarters of the 13th Coast Artillery Regiment and the Harbor Defenses of Pensacola. Small army posts at both Fort Pickens and Fort McRee supported the active gun batteries of the 13th Coast Artillery Regiment in the 1930s and 1940s, while members of the National Guard and ROTC students came to Fort Pickens for their training on antiaircraft and heavy artillery. The U.S. Army also maintained a small unit on Horn Island in 1943.

By 1947, with the war over, the four remaining forts were reclassified as "surplus." Local efforts came together in the 1960s to preserve these forts and the pristine beaches that connect them, as well as the fragile wilderness islands off the coasts of Florida, Alabama, and Mississippi. The concept of a national seashore—a protected wilderness with significant historical value—became the clear way to solve the preservation issues while creating a recreation area for people from all over the world to enjoy. In 1971, President Richard M. Nixon signed into law the bill that created Gulf Islands National Seashore, the nation's largest.

Fort Barrancas became the headquarters of the 13th Coast Artillery Regiment.

Flora and Fauna:
All Things Great and Small

The Gulf Islands serve as a haven for migrating and nesting birds, a home for tiny shellfish and larger sea creatures, and a place for dolphins to play and an occasional manatee to swim in safety. Its concentrated forest areas provide shelter and food for armadillos, raccoons, and opossum, and its undisturbed beaches allow sea turtles to nest in relatively protected comfort. Complete with sub-tropical plant life, fragrant magnolias, and all manner of flowering-trees and shrubs, the Gulf Islands are a naturalist's paradise.

Birds by the Flock

Sanderlings running to and fro along the waterline, willets strutting solo as they plunge their bills deep into the sand, ruddy turnstones clustering at the wrack line to dig out tiny shellfish—all of these

◄ *A monarch butterfly feeds on common strawberry.*

Larger than a sanderling, a willet strolls on the edge of the surf.

shorebirds are year-round residents of the Gulf Islands. For an excellent look at all of these common species—and a chance to see some of the less-common beachcombing birds—drive to the east end of Perdido Key, park, and walk out onto the empty beach, where few people go and birds are most comfortable.

Black skimmers and endangered piping plovers nest on the beaches, a choice that may have been safe a century ago, before the beach became a favorite recreation area for millions of people annually. Today, the crowds on the beaches during nesting season place the birds' shallowly sheltered eggs in a precarious position. The birds make small depressions in the sand and lay their sand-colored eggs in them, making these nests virtually undetectable to the casual passerby . . . and therefore in grave danger of being trampled. Please respect their nesting areas, which are clearly posted and roped off by the park staff. (You're welcome to stand outside of these areas and scan with binoculars for any recently hatched birds. Look for the

Great Florida Birding Trail signs.)

Any time of year, scan the skies over the Gulf of Mexico for brown pelicans, royal and sandwich terns, Forster's tern, and the plucky least tern, a tiny white bird with a black cap and a rapid, swooping flight pattern. Laughing gulls are the most common, easily spotted with their black caps in spring and summer, and their speckled heads and black "eyeliner" in winter. Ring-billed and herring gulls round out the mixed flocks you'll find on the beaches, especially near any group of people in the midst of a picnic. (Feeding these birds is illegal; if you're caught, you'll pay a hefty fine.)

It's easy to see great blue herons, great and snowy egrets, and yellow-crowned night herons at this seashore.

Great egrets often perch in trees near water.

Try the Santa Rosa Sound beach area at the Naval Live Oaks visitor center, where the narrow ribbon of damp sand attracts herons and egrets, as well as feeding shorebirds and terns. Check in the marsh grasses along the shoreline for night herons, green herons, and the occasional tricolored heron.

There's spectacular water birding at Davis Bayou, on the Mississippi end of the park. Take the road to the campgrounds, on the way to the self-interpreted nature trail, and park just before the causeway over the salt marsh. You can walk out onto this bridge and scan the marsh grass, mudflats, and inlets to the north and south for herons, egrets, shorebirds, and ducks; in particular, hooded and red-breasted mergansers, American coot, and common moorhen winter here, while lesser scaup and blue-winged teal are common in spring and fall. Belted kingfishers make this part

of the bayou their home, announcing their approach with their rattling, percussive calls.

Shy, secretive clapper rails may be easy to find in Davis Bayou, if you're willing to stand quietly on a wooden platform overlooking a salt marsh while the tide is low. These skulking creatures sometimes show themselves toward dusk, picking their way along the edge of a mudflat where cordgrass offers instant concealment. Your slightest movement will scare this chicken-like bird back into cover, so be as still as you can.

In the wooded areas of Naval Live Oaks and Davis Bayou, spring brings a riot of colorful, chirping birds on their way to breeding habitat to the north. Virtually all of the eastern warblers

Ruby-crowned kinglets winter in the Gulf Islands.

are certain to see northern mockingbird, tufted titmouse, mourning dove, northern cardinal, Carolina chickadee, Carolina wren, and downy, hairy, and red-bellied woodpeckers, all of which are year-round residents.

The northern mockingbird sings from every woods.

may stop here to recover from the Gulf crossing, so your list may include orange-crowned, Nashville, Blackburnian, palm, pine, yellow-throated, bay-breasted, worm-eating, Swainson's, and cerulean warblers, as well as the more common yellow-rumped and black-and-white warblers. You

Armadillos rustle in the leaves on the forest floor.

Eyes in the Woods

That rustling you hear under the leaves in the heart of the bayou or along a trail near Fort Pickens could be a nine-banded armadillo, hunting for insects beneath the understory. These highly entertaining animals, covered from nose to tail in a leathery shell, are not always easy to find: Listen for their progress through low brush and last year's leaves, especially on a day when winds are calm.

Raccoons, opossum, gray squirrels, and skunks may reveal themselves in wooded areas, while eastern cottontail rabbits often put in appearances along forest edges. In Mississippi, you're very likely to spot a nutria, an invasive water-loving rodent species (often referred to as "nutria rat") that was imported into Louisiana in the 1930s from South America. They feed voraciously on wetland plants, making them a destructive influence on marsh habitat—and they breed with equal enthusiasm. Efforts are in the works to control the increase in nutria populations; in the meantime, they're interesting to watch as they wander the marshes and chow down on various plants.

The most-talked-about land mammal in the national seashore, however, is the Perdido Key beach mouse, a tiny, nocturnal creature you are very unlikely to spot. The beach mouse landed on the endangered species list in 1985 and its numbers continue to dwindle as its habitat falls to commercial development. Driven nearly to extinction in the mid-1990s by hurricanes Erin and Opal, the mice managed to recover, with about 500 individuals estimated recently. The tiny mice—each weighing less than half an ounce—make their home in the vegetation in the dunes on or near Perdido Key.

Life between Land and Sea

Visit the beach at low tide and walk along the waterline, and you will definitely see seashells—but you may also see shells with their inhabitants firmly entrenched and alive. Fiddler crabs may wave to you from tiny holes, especially along wet mudflats in the park's marshes. Calico scallops, conch, and whelk shells may wash up on the beach, but if you see a snail shell, be careful when you pick it up: It may contain a hermit crab, a wily crustacean that borrows another creature's shell and moves in. Horseshoe crabs, actually a member of the spider family, wait quietly in their helmet-like shells for the next tide to pull them back into the water—so if the shell you find has a tail, let it be.

Fiddler crabs emerge from holes in mudflats.

You won't find as many shells on the Mississippi end of the seashore, but on the wilderness islands, look along the shoreline for ghost crabs, weirdly white crustaceans that prefer the remote islands to the mainland shores. Mole crabs and southern coquina—multicolored clams with a triangular shell—are easy to spot on island beaches.

Davis Bayou provides exactly the right habitat for American alligators, those 5- to 7-foot reptiles with the crooked teeth rimming their formidable jaws. One of the best places to see them is from the platform just across the road from the 0.5-mile nature trail in the bayou (see the map, page 59), where alligators often laze along the bank of this wetland.

You may glimpse an alligator—or part of one—in the Mississippi bayou.

The Sea Turtle: A Struggle to Survive

The national seashore is famous for its variety of turtles, including sea turtles, which lay their eggs on the beach in holes they dig in the sand. The female sea turtle may lay as many as 160 eggs per nest, covering them with sand before she returns to the sea. Sun on the sand warms the eggs, and two months later, the hatchlings appear at night, digging their way out of the nest and moving toward the brightest light they see. If they're on a wilderness beach somewhere far from civilization, the moon or stars reflected on the water would serve as the bright light—but here on the edge of cities, the lights from buildings and backyards attract the hatchlings, drawing them away from the water. These tiny turtles then become food for many animals, or they end up in streets and are run over by cars. In the end, only one in a thousand actually survives.

National park volunteers join the "turtle watch" every spring, often sitting up all night next to a turtle nest to help direct the hatchlings toward the water. Thanks to these devoted amateur naturalists and their leaders at the national seashore, more turtles make it through this critical phase after hatching—and if you keep an eye out, you may well see them swimming close to shore.

Beautyberry's purple fruit is especially striking.

Spectacular Flowers and Berries

Magnolia blooming in the forests, red basil sending up stalks crowned with scarlet flowers, golden aster nodding in the breeze, alternating with low-growing saw palmetto—these are the blooms of the national seashore's woods. From March until well into November, you can enjoy all kinds of flowering plants as well as a fascinating variety of shrubs and native trees found only in this region.

Have you ever seen beautyberry? This extraordinarily violet berry, growing in great clusters on shrubs up to 6 feet high, is the fruit that results after tiny lavender blossoms cover these twigs in June. The berries are edible but very bitter.

Spanish moss hangs from live oaks and other trees.

Slash pines fill the gaps between stately live oaks, all draped in Spanish moss and forming a canopy over a variety of shrubs and herbs. Groundsel trees with puffballs of white flowers are particularly striking next to the bright red berries of the yaupon holly, a hardy southern species that bears no other resemblance to the holly of snow-dusted northern forests.

The landscape changes dramatically as we move from forest to open marsh, where needlerush and cordgrass are the tallest plants and wide vistas replace the dense woods.

Each new bend brings a world of visual delights, whether the view is the open beach, woodlands thick with vegetation, salt marshes stretching to the horizon, or vistas across island sands.

Horizons:
Natural and Historic Sites

Whether you seek clues to America's military might or the seclusion of white-sand islands, you'll find your heart's desire at this seashore.

Naval Live Oaks

Walk the Brackenridge Nature Trail, a 0.8-mile loop trail that begins at the Naval Live Oaks visitor center, and see the eerily twisted live oak trees; 1,300 acres remain of the original 60,000-acre timber preserve. Naval live oaks served the U.S. Navy nobly until the late nineteenth century, when more-powerful weapons rendered wooden ships obsolete. The USS *Constitution* (now docked in Boston) was built with live oak, and earned its nickname, "Old Ironsides," when cannonballs bounced off its tough wooden sides.

As you walk this delightful trail, note the interpretive signs that

◀ *Davis Bayou forms an ecosystem around fresh- and salt water.*

illustrate the various ship parts that could be cut from the trees' expansive trunks and branches.

Davis Bayou

This Mississippi salt marsh is actually an estuary, in which freshwater enters through runoff from streams, and saltwater comes in on the tides. Hardy grasses dominate this dynamic environment, making homes for many small creatures that find a food source here as the marsh grasses begin to decay. This 470-acre preserve serves as the nurturing ground for many shelled creatures, including the annual shrimp migration: As the salinity of the water changes, different shrimp species are attracted to the area, coming here to feed on the nutrient-rich soup

The roots of sea oats help stabilize the wilderness islands.

created by the confluence of water, land, and plant life—and when the salinity level lowers in the wet season, the shrimp will move out to sea.

Explore this area on foot by taking the 0.5-mile Nature's Way interpretive trail, just across the bayou from the

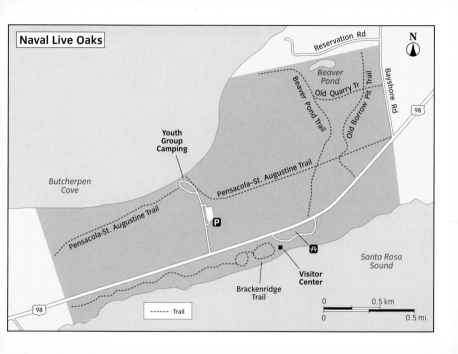

picnic area and campground. Pick up the trail brochure from the holder at the trailhead, and learn about small changes in elevation and what they mean to the wildlife and foliage.

West Ship Island

Take the Ship Island Excursions ferry from Gulfport, Mississippi (see page 7), and discover West Ship Island, 11 miles off the Mississippi coast and one of the last truly unspoiled barrier islands on the northwestern Gulf Coast. Wiped nearly clean of its visitor amenities by Hurricane Katrina in 2005, much of this island has returned to its natural state, and the emerald waters lapping at the pure white beach will make you wish you could stay well beyond the last ferry's departure.

The only remaining structure is Fort Massachusetts (more on this below), and a .33-mile boardwalk that ends at the swimming beach. Shade shelters, restrooms, a ranger residence, and snack bar are also found here.

Known for its excellent year-round birding, with breeding species including least and royal terns and black skimmers, West Ship Island offers fun beachcombing for hermit crabs and occasional starfish—but any live marine life or inhabited shells you find must be left alone. Ranger programs include natural history walks and historical interpretive tours of the fort.

Horn and Petit Bois Islands

Only a few places in the eastern United States can offer a taste of true wilder-ess, and the Gulf Islands has two ederally protected wilderness islands: orn and Petit Bois (pronounced 'etty Boy") Islands. Take one of the ark-approved charter boat services or your own boat, if you have experience in ocean waters) and cross Mississippi Sound to see dramatic andscapes of wind-sculpted dunes, eld together by the stems and roots f tenacious sea oats, sand pines, nd saw palmetto. No visitor services xist on either island, so you'll have e pleasure of walking the circumference of an island on unbroken sand, or rossing the islands on trails—much s famed artist Walter Anderson did when he spent weeks at a time on this emote island to paint and write.

Petit Bois Island's vegetation includes fewer trees than you'll find on Horn Island, providing us with a sense of the fragility of this landscape. Changing with each year's storms, this natural panorama invites repeated exploration, an opportunity to examine the effects of nature's forces as they alter the scene from one season to the next.

Fort Pickens

It took 21.5 million bricks to construct the largest of the national seashore's forts, but today Fort Pickens stands up to the fiercest hurricane winds and storm surges—a fitting tribute to the slave crews who labored here. The fort faced combat only twice, serving as a stronghold for Union troops in November 1861 and January 1862 as they bombarded the Confederate army on the mainland. In the end, the Union triumphed—but only after attacks elsewhere that drove the southern army to abandon the area at last in May 1862.

A visit to the fort today reveals nearly 200 years of American military history. As bigger and more power-

A powder magazine explosion tore through the walls of Fort Pickens.

ful guns and explosives made brick construction obsolete, the U.S. Army Corps of Engineers added Battery Pensacola in 1898, equipping the new fortification with 12-inch guns mounted on disappearing carriages. (Nine additional batteries in the Fort Pickens area were built to maintain coastal defenses.) Not long after the installation of Battery Pensacola, a fire in a storeroom ignited more than 8,000 pounds of black powder, blowing the fort's northwest wall sky-high and showering debris for more than a mile and a half. The wall has never been repaired, so you can see the results of the blast's impressive force.

Take a ranger-led tour (offered daily at 2:00 p.m.), or explore on your own with the help of the brochure you'll find at the fort's entrance.

Fort Barrancas / Advanced Redoubt

If a fort can be beautiful, Fort Barrancas certainly is; the extraordinary masonry work here, especially in the scarp gallery, takes fort design to a new level of ingenuity, usability, and aesthetics. More than six million bricks went into the construction of the 4-foot-thick walls and startlingly graceful arches, and each element of the fort demonstrates sound military strategy: The dry moat could stop invaders in their tracks as 130 guns opened fire through rifle slits in the wall; gunners had the ability to heat 24-pound cannonballs and load them into 5,000-pound cannons, to fire them at attacking ships.

Like Fort Pickens, Barrancas only

The designers of Fort Barrancas took aesthetics seriously.

saw combat during a short period of the Civil War, but it remained on active duty as a training base until 1947. Tour the fort and the adjoining Water Battery, a defensive structure constructed by the Spanish in the late 1700s. You will walk through an underground tunnel to the battery, a route repaired by the Works Progress Administration in the 1930s.

Seven hundred yards north of Fort Barrancas stands the Advanced Redoubt, an additional fortification built over a twenty-five-year period, from 1845 to 1870. Constructed specifically to defend the northern side of the peninsula and the navy yard, the Advanced Redoubt demonstrates a well-considered military strategy: By the time attacking troops fought their way through the redoubt's multiple defenses, they would lose strength and momentum, placing them at serious risk.

Tours here are self-guided during the week with a brochure you will find

Walk through a dark tunnel to the Water Battery.

at the Fort Barrancas Visitor Center. Guided tours are given at 11:00 a.m. on Saturdays. Check at the visitor center for other scheduled ranger programs in summer.

Fort Massachusetts

Twelve miles off the Mississippi coast on West Ship Island, Fort Massachusetts proved to be the most difficult of the Gulf Coast's forts to construct; in fact, it was never truly finished. Yet the United States military saw this strategic island point as one of the most important areas to protect, because it had actually been used in the British invasion of New Orleans in 1814, serving as a gathering place for 10,000 attacking troops. Even more important, New Orleans' shipping lanes passed near Ship Island, putting a critical import and export route at risk.

The Civil War interrupted the fort's construction, however, as Confederates seized the island. When Union troops took it back, Admiral David Farragut staged his attack on New Orleans from here in 1862; later, the island became a prisoner-of-war camp where the 74th Regiment U.S. Colored Troops, originally known as the 2nd Louisiana Native Guards, guarded the Confederate prisoners. By 1901, the military scrapped the fort and its limited weaponry, with the exception of its 15-inch Rodman cannon, the only cannon in the national seashore that's still on its original mount.

Visiting the fort requires a ferry ride out to West Ship Island, where you can go out with a ranger or tour on your own.

Pensacola Lighthouse

Officially owned by the U.S. Coast Guard, Pensacola Lighthouse is within the legislative boundaries of Gulf Islands National Seashore. You'll find this impressive light on Pensacola Naval Air Station, standing near the site on which the original structure was built in 1824. This 171-foot tower replaced it in 1858.

The lighthouse survived the Civil War, numerous lightning strikes, countless tropical storms, and even an earthquake before the end of the nineteenth century, and once electricity was installed in 1930, automation quickly followed. A 1965 preservation effort brings us the opportunity to enjoy this tall beacon today.

For more information on available tours, call the Pensacola Lighthouse Association at (850) 944-0179 or (850) 916-7864, or visit on a Saturday from 2:00 to 4:00 p.m., May through Octo-

This Pensacola Lighthouse was built in 1858. ▶

ber. You'll find more information about the lighthouse at www.lighthouse friends.com.

Get Going:
Activities in the Park

Your Gulf Coast adventure can take place on land or sea, along the coast or deep in the woods, under your own power or by land vehicle or boat—but whatever way you choose to enjoy Gulf Islands National Seashore, you're sure to find new places to explore and plenty of activity to fill your days.

Go to the Beach!

You'll hear everyone say it: "Sugar-white sands and emerald green water" are the hallmarks of Gulf Islands' beaches. Choose from Fort Pickens Beach on the west end of Santa Rosa Island, or take the ferry to West Ship Island; or cross through Pensacola to picturesque Perdido Key—or pick a spot anywhere between the park entrances and these lifeguard-protected beaches for a secluded seashore

◀ *Marshes and bayous offer great paddling experiences.*

Beach Warning Flags Tell an Important Story

Check the flags at designated beach swim areas to be sure it's a great day for swimming. Even a bright, blue-sky day can bring brisk winds that kick up the surf.

The National Park Service posts warning flags to let you know what the conditions are, and what precautions you may need to take. You'll see these flags flying over every beach entrance on Santa Rosa Island and at Perdido Key, including those at Pensacola Beach; there's even a colored flag just as you enter the island over the bridge from the mainland, to let you know how "up" the surf may be.

Here's the simple code, to help you recognize the conditions at a glance:

Green: Low hazard, calm conditions; exercise caution.

Yellow: Medium hazard, moderate surf and/or currents.

Red: High hazard, high surf and/or strong currents.

Red over red: Beach is closed to the public.

Purple: Dangerous marine life.

You may see the purple flag flying even on a calm day—and "dangerous" can mean an influx of jellyfish or stingrays, the appearance of sea nettles, or . . . yes, even a shark. There hasn't been a shark attack incident here since 2001, but some sharks do migrate through these waters, so take the purple flag seriously.

Ask a ranger or lifeguard if you have any questions.

experience away from the crowds. In Mississippi, take the ferry to West Ship Island and relax on its wind-swept shoreline (you can rent a beach umbrella and chaise, but there are no other services on the island), or use your own boat or a charter to motor to Horn or Petit Bois Islands, for wide stretches of beach all to yourself.

The warm Gulf waters are at their best from March through October, although beach days are possible even in November and February, when bright blue skies can bring temperate days. You'll enjoy long walks along the shore-line any time of year, and when summer heat shimmers against the white sand, there's nothing like a refreshing plunge in some of the clearest water you'll find at a national seashore.

Enjoy beachcombing and walks on the sand.

Even if you don't choose to play in the evergreen waters, beachcomb-ing along the Gulf of Mexico can yield all kinds of marine riches. Fully intact shells from scallops, crabs, whelks, conch, snails, and clams all wash up on the shore. You're welcome to take empty, uninhabited shells home with you, but limit your load to what you can carry (it's okay to fill up a sand pail).

Some good tips for a beach day: Wear sunscreen; bring insect repellent; drink plenty of water; and wear a hat to protect your head from the intense Florida sunshine. As you splash into the Gulf, shuffle your feet to keep from stepping on stingrays, which can hide in loose sand at the sea bottom.

Easy, Level Hiking in Natural Surroundings

Pleasant nature walks along boardwalks and interpreted trails, long-distance hikes across miles of uninterrupted beach, or narrow paths through tightly interwoven shrubs and vines—whatever your personal hiking preference, you'll find your new favorite hikes here among Gulf Islands' three mainland units.

Beaver Pond Trail in the Naval Live Oaks area takes you through a mile's worth of southeastern forest, with slash pine, magnolia, and saw palmetto crowding one another all along the path's perimeter. You may see a pile of mud, twigs, and scrubby brush packed together in Brown's Pond—the work of the industrious southern beavers. Extend your hike by veering right on the Brown's Pond trail and circling the pond, returning on Reservation Road and retracing your route down Beaver Pond trail.

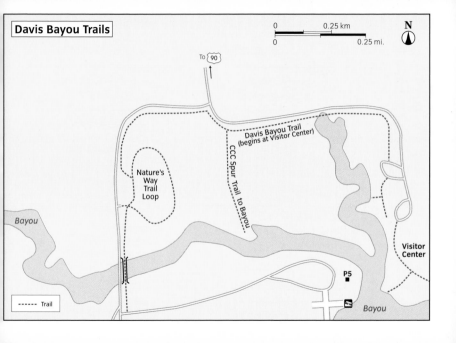

Davis Bayou Trails

0   0.25 km

0   0.25 mi.

N

To 90

Davis Bayou Trail (begins at Visitor Center)

CCC Spur Trail to Bayou

Nature's Way Trail Loop

Bayou

Visitor Center

P5

Bayou

------- Trail

The 2.4-mile (one way) Andrew Jackson Trail crosses the Naval Live Oaks unit from one end to the other, making this an all-afternoon hike if you walk out and back. Formerly a section of the 1824-built Pensacola-St. Augustine Road, this trail now takes you into the live oak preserve for a sense of the wilderness that once covered the panhandle. Hikers may park at the lot near the maintenance compound on the north side of US 98.

If you're thinking about through-hiking one of the country's eight National Scenic Trails, you've come to the right place: Florida National Scenic Trail (NST) begins at Fort Pickens, and

Walking the Florida National Scenic Trail may reveal hurricane damage to the old Fort Pickens Road.

28.2 miles of the trail cross Gulf Islands National Seashore. From the fort, walk the old oyster-shell path to the beach, and then walk along the shoreline through Pensacola Beach to the dunes and coastal scrub of Navarre Beach. Once you've reached Navarre Beach Park, you can continue to follow the Florida NST by crossing the causeway to the mainland and turning east on the causeway. More information, including detailed maps for this 1,300-mile trail—which extends from here to Big Cypress National Preserve in South Florida—is available at www.floridatrail.org.

In Mississippi, explore the Davis Bayou Trail, a 1-mile walk through a coastal forest and across two bayous. You'll connect with the Nature's Way Loop Trail, an interpreted route with some slight changes in elevation that completely alter the kinds of plants and animals that make this wilderness their home. This easy, pleasant walk gives hikers a thorough overview of the bayou's idiosyncratic ecosystem, with the possibility of spotting kingfishers, yellow-rumped warblers, and a clapper rail scurrying out of view along the edge of a mudflat.

Biking on Paved, Level Pathways

The interconnections between the national seashore and neighboring towns make for some long, wonderful bicycle routes, with bike lanes on public roads, and long stretches of paved trails that feature outstanding views of the seashore, sound, and bayou.

The South Santa Rosa Loop Trail offers a nearly 40-mile ride beginning at Navarre Beach Nature Walk, crossing Santa Rosa Island to the west, and continuing through Pensacola Beach to the bridge to Gulf Breeze. Cross the bridge and turn right on US 98, and continue east on the highway through the Naval Live Oaks unit and beyond, until you reach the bridge to Navarre. When you cross the bridge, you'll be close to your starting point at Navarre Beach Nature Walk. The loop trail showcases some of the Gulf Islands' most lovely habitats, including long sweeps of dune-lined beach, fragrant foliage loaded with blooms, and huge live oaks.

In Ocean Springs, the Live Oaks Bicycle Route winds its way for just over 7 miles along the town's roads, with green and white bike route signs and a bike lane on most main roads. Beginning at the L&N Train Depot, a 1907 building on the National Register of Historic Places, the route travels through downtown Ocean Springs to the Walter Anderson Museum, and on through the town's historic district and beaches. Later, you'll pass the Gulf Coast Research Laboratory before entering Davis Bayou and the national seashore. The route ends at the boat ramp pavilion in the bayou. Turn around here and retrace the route for a total ride of 15.5 miles.

Go Fishing

Whether you charter a boat and go out into deep water, stay on land and fish from the Fort Pickens pier, or cast a net for shellfish in a sea-grass bed, you'll find fishing in the Gulf Islands especially rewarding. Flounder, bull reds, speckled sea trout, and Spanish mackerel are just a few of the plentiful specialties in these waters, and you can net and gather shrimp, crabs, oysters, and scallops (there's no commercial fishing allowed). The Resources section at the back of the book lists some fishing charters and guides who can take you to the best areas for deep-sea fishing, while park staff members can direct you to great areas for spearfishing and netting. (For information on sources for fishing licenses in Florida and Mississippi, see page 16.)

Just for Families

When you've built all the sand villages you can handle and you've filled your pockets with shells, you and your family may be ready for a different kind of adventure. Gulf Islands National Seashore offers plenty of opportunities to sneak a little nature lesson in between your days on the beach, with interpreted trails across dunes and through forests, entertaining and informative ranger programs, and the chance to earn a badge or patch while having lots of fun in the park.

Be a Junior Ranger or a Sea Star

Stop at any of the park visitor centers and pick up a Junior Ranger Activity Book for children ages six to eleven, or a Sea Star book for three- to five-year-olds. By completing a certain number of activities in the booklet (the number is based on the child's age), visiting a park museum, attending a ranger program, walking a nature trail,

◀ *You'll find plenty of easy family walks in the Gulf Islands.*

and picking up at least ten pieces of trash for proper disposal, children can earn a Junior Ranger Certificate of Completion and a badge. There's no cost for the booklet or any of the activities, and everyone in the family can participate in the program.

Very young children can become Seashore Sea Stars by completing activities in their own age-appropriate booklet. Coloring a flower pink, checking things they see in the park on a list in the booklet, or drawing a spiderweb are just a few of the choices provided in the book, making the day in the park educational as well as fun.

In the Mississippi District, June and July are special months for Junior Rangers: If your child attends four ranger programs during these months, he or she receives a free round-trip pass to ride the ferry to West Ship Island. Check at the Colmer Visitor Center in Davis Bayou for more information. In Florida, Junior Ranger day camps are held throughout the summer and on several school holidays; ask for information at the Naval Live Oaks or Fort Pickens visitor centers.

Rangers Lead Great Adventures

Take a walk on a barrier island, see what birds arrived overnight in the salt marshes, explore the dunes, or see what crabs look like, all by joining a ranger-led program throughout the year. Rangers know where to find the "good stuff" among the ponds, mudflats, marsh edges, and gulf shore, giving you some of the best opportunities at the seashore to see wildlife up close or to find an animal or bird you've never seen before.

If you'd like to learn more about what life was like as a soldier or prisoner in one of the seashore's old brick forts, tour the fort with a ranger as your guide. Well versed in military history and experts at telling wonderful stories about the people who lived, worked, and fought here, the rangers can open your eyes to facets of fort life that you may not have discovered on your own.

Check online at www.nps.gov/guis/planyourvisit/events.htm for events and programs scheduled during your upcoming visit, or stop at a visitor center and pick up a list of programs when you arrive at the park.

Easy Hikes for Short Legs

Whether you're planning a day at Rosamond Johnson Beach at Perdido Key, picnicking in the shadow of Fort Barrancas, or venturing into the Mississippi bayou, you'll find an interpreted trail close by that will delight walkers of all ages.

The **Woodland Nature Trail** at Fort Barrancas, a 0.5-mile loop, leads you on a leisurely stroll through a forest in recovery, where sand pine saplings are taking root and replacing those destroyed by the 2004 and 2005 hurricanes. Sturdy live oaks draped in Spanish moss remain erect, just as they have for hundreds of years, and

Walk the boardwalk on the Perdido Key Discovery Trail .

A 0.25-mile boardwalk amble, the uncommonly pleasant Perdido Key Discovery Trail provides access to three different habitats: salt marsh, naturally sculpted dunes, and maritime forest. Loblolly pine and southern red cedar skirt the edge of the marsh and find footing beyond the dunes, while sea oats and sandspurs work to hold the dunes in place. Here you'll find expanses of salt-tolerant plants like rosemary, groundsel, and yaupon holly, creating a wild landscape of dark, fragrant green against bright, light-reflective white sand. The marsh overlook, just beyond the parking lot at the trailhead, can be a good vantage point for long-legged birds, frogs, and turtles.

turkey oak—with bright red leaves in the fall—stands strong even in the wake of major storms.

Hey Ranger! Q&A Just For Kids

Q. What is a bayou?

A. A bayou starts out as a tributary of a larger body of water, like a lake or a river. Something slows it down, though—maybe from a shift in the soil that cuts it off from its original river, or a change in the elevation of the surrounding land. The water becomes sluggish, or it may stop moving altogether, and the land becomes swampy. Bayous are an important part of the Gulf of Mexico's coastline because they help drain water off of the mainland after a major storm floods the area.

Q. Why are there two Ship Islands?

A. There used to be just one Ship Island, until Hurricane Camille came in 1969. When that huge storm blew through, it had reached Category 5 strength with winds of 190 miles per hour, making it one of the worst storms ever to come to the Gulf Islands in recorded history. All that force washed all the sand out of a low area toward the middle of the island, and the big gap filled with water, creating a channel between the two halves. This wasn't the first time Ship Island had been split in two. But while it had been able to heal itself after past storms, this time the channel is too deep, and park rangers say they don't expect the two halves to come back together.

Recharge:
Places to Sleep and Eat

Gulf Islands seashore has no historic lodges, restaurants, or other indoor accommodations in the park, but camping opportunities here range from the civilized—with electrical hookups and showers—to primitive areas on wilderness islands.

Fort Pickens's 200-site campground features electrical hookups and standpipes at every site, as well as a picnic table and grill. Restrooms feature flush toilets and hot showers, making this a particularly pleasant place to camp. The sites are $20 per night—but holders of the America the Beautiful National Parks and Federal Recreational Lands *Senior* and *Access* passes (not the standard Annual Pass) receive a 50 percent discount on nightly camping rates.

In Ocean Springs, the 51-site Davis Bayou Campground is open to both tent campers and recreational vehicles. The sites provide

◀ *The park provides tent and RV camping in both Florida and Mississippi.*

running water and electricity, and the RV sites can accommodate a trailer that is up to 45 feet in length. The restrooms have hot showers. Sites are available on a first come, first served basis, and each site is $16 per night.

For an entirely different kind of camping experience, go primitive and take a boat out to Horn, Petit Bois, East Ship, or Cat Islands, where you and your family may have the entire island all to yourselves. Of course, you'll need to bring your own food, water, and supplies, as there are no services at all to be found on these islands, and insect repellent and mosquito netting are vital if you want to sleep comfortably in this wilderness setting. Build a fire on the beach below the high-tide line and enjoy a night offshore, surrounded by turquoise waters and open air.

In Florida, on the eastern end of Perdido Key, you can walk half a mile through soft sand beyond the end of the paved road and camp at land's end, pitching your tent wherever you please. Register at the Perdido Key Ranger Station and pick up a copy of the rules for primitive camping before setting out. You'll need to bring all of your own supplies, as the nearest services are outside the park at the other end of the key.

Camp on the unspoiled beach at the end of Perdido Key.

Beyond the Borders:
Off-site Places to Sleep, Eat, and Go

Your visit to Gulf Islands National Seashore is almost certain to include a stay in either Pensacola Beach, Florida, or Ocean Springs, Mississippi, two towns determined to provide a true escape from the daily trials of mainland life.

On the edge of the immaculate shore, the town of Pensacola Beach delivers an experience as deliciously opposite to real life as visitors could wish. Luxury condominiums—available for a night, a week, or the whole summer—offer spa treatments, huge indoor and outdoor pools, and boutique shopping, while restaurants fill your plate with fresh selections from the day's catch. Sample a bushwhacker (a whipped-up concoction involving Kahlua, dark rum, cream of coconut, crème de cacao, and milk), munch some deep-fried alligator (which tastes like whatever sauce you dip it in,

◄ *Pensacola Beach is as much fun at night as it is by day.*

and not much else), or crack open a boiled crab, all while gazing out toward the Gulf of Mexico as the sun dips below the horizon.

Where to Stay in Pensacola Beach

Choose a hotel if you're only staying a few days, or rent an apartment or a condo—but no matter what time of year you plan to arrive, be sure to book early, as increases in year-round tourism have made Pensacola Beach a major attraction in all four seasons.

Newly remodeled with laser-focused attention to detail, the **Holiday Inn Express** (formerly the Dunes Hotel) goes well beyond the chain for-

There's no missing the turn to Pensacola Beach.

nat to provide a resort-quality experi-ence, with a Gulf view in every room, a West Indies sensibility in the rattan and wood furnishings, and an outdoor breakfast patio—with a complimen-ary full, hot breakfast—overlooking he beach. Ask about the executive ing suites, with balconies that offer some of the best views on the beach. Prices range from $210 to $290 in season, $140 to $220 off-season; call or suite rates; 333 Fort Pickens Road, 850) 932-3536, www.hiexpress.com.

If you're looking for a dream vacation experience with all of the luxuries of the Florida coast, choose **Portofino Island Resort,** a 28-acre vacation condominium complex at the very edge of the seashore's protected and. Rising high over both the Gulf of Mexico and Santa Rosa Sound, Portofino's towers offer fully furnished two- and three-bedroom apartments and plenty of on-site and nearby activi-ties to entertain adults and children. Amenities include daily setup of your beach chair and umbrella, DVD movie rentals, use of the on-site fitness center, transportation to shopping in Pensacola Beach, and—perhaps best of all—a daily round of golf on any of four Emerald Coast Golf Trail courses. Prices range from $260 to $280/day for a two-bedroom condo off-season, $460 to $480 in summer, plus resort fees; 10 Portofino Drive, (888) 707-0945, www.PortofinoIsland.com.

A more cost-conscious choice is the newly remodeled **Paradise Inn,** a spotlessly clean motel on the shore of

Santa Rosa Sound. King, queen, and two- and three-bed rooms accommodate families with children, and pets are welcome (for a fee). Microwave ovens and refrigerators in each room, continental breakfast, outdoor pool, and easy beach access make this a good, economical choice. There's a popular bar and grill on the premises as well. Prices range from $70 to $100 off-season, $100 to $150 and up in the summer (call for daily specials); 21 Via De Luna Drive, (850) 932-2319 or (800) 301-5925, www.paradiseinn-pb.com.

Of the brand-name hotels, it's no surprise that the **Hilton Pensacola Beach Gulf Front** rises to the top. This luxury hotel sports a seventeen-story, all-suites tower in which virtually every room has a water view. Suites offer bedrooms with two queen beds, bunk beds for children, and balconies that face the sunset. In the lobby, the H2O Grill serves a continental or full hot breakfast daily (not included in your room price), and switches to "Cajun Asian" fusion fare for lunch and dinner. Rooms start at $120 in the off-season, $170 in season (call for current rates); 12 Via De Luna Drive, (866) 916-2999, www.pensacolabeach.stayhgi.com.

The new **Hampton Inn Pensacola Beach Gulf Front** is the latest addition to the Highpointe Hotel Corporation's high-quality collection, which also includes the nearby Springhill Suites and Days Inn. Enjoy a complimentary breakfast or an afternoon with a good book on the spacious, sunny outdoor deck, or take a dip in the pool. When

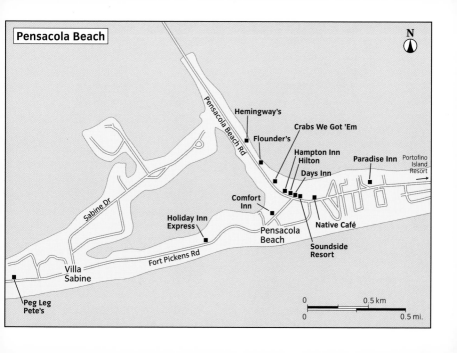

the sun's over the yardarm, stop at Gilligan's Beachside Tiki Bar for a tropical beverage. Prices range from $100 to $160 off-season, $180 to $300 in summer; 2 Via de Luna, (850) 932-6800, www.hamptonbeachresort.com.

Where to Eat in Pensacola Beach

Seafood? They've got that—and plenty of choices for meat eaters as well. It's easy to find a great meal at a reasonable price on this island, and there's no shortage of places to stand, sit, or lean and enjoy the summer breezes with a daiquiri or a piña colada.

Crabs We Got 'Em, 6 Casino Beach Boulevard, Gulf Breeze, (850) 932-0700, www.crabswegotem.com. How big a stack of Alaska snow crab clus-

ters can you eat? This is the place to find out: Lit with festive twinkle lights, the upstairs beach-view dining room is usually jammed with guests tackling stacks of king crab legs or straying just a bit from the theme to devour shrimp scampi conchiglie, a luscious pasta dish involving local shrimp, raw garlic, and Alfredo sauce. Nightly bar specials on the outdoor deck, baskets of fried seafood, and enormous platters will satisfy you for days to come. Entrees range from $18 to $30 (prices may vary seasonally).

Flounder's Chowder House, 800 Quietwater Beach Road, (850) 932-2003, www.flounderschowderhouse.com. It's been voted "best seafood restaurant" in local polls for good reason—Flounder's combines terrific

How much key lime pie do you need? Find out at Flounder's.

food with a merry atmosphere. You **must** start with the baked oysters Pensacola—oysters, cheese, crumbs, garlic, and parsley baked crunchy on the outside, sweet and tender underneath. Your fish comes straight from the gulf in your favorite style: blackened, almandine, bourbon-glazed, or with citrus beurre blanc. Order just

one serving of the triple-stacked key lime pie—it's enough for a table of four to share. Open for lunch, dinner, and late-night meals, with entrees ranging from $15 to $25, and salads, po' boys, and burgers, from $10 to $12.

Hemingway's Island Grill, 400 Quietwater Beach Road, #16, (850) 934-4747, www.ernesthemingway collection.com (click on "hospitality"). The most creative restaurant on the beach, this fine establishment's sweeping ceiling fans, huge windows, and breezy dining room inspire wistful thoughts of the iconic author who lived much larger than life. The exciting menu pairs pork tenderloin with mango sauce, calamari with honey chipotle glaze, and traditional Caesar salad with a coconut-pineapple dressing—just enough off the beaten path to tickle your palate. Open for lunch and dinner, with dinner entrees ranging from $13 to $26; lunch, $8 to $12.

McGuire's Irish Pub, 600 East Gregory Street, Pensacola, (850) 433-6789, www.mcguiresirishpub.com. Just over the bridge from the beach in Pensacola, this is the steak house and pub that every local resident recommended. They were right—from the bowl of bean soup for 18 cents (really!) to the steaks sizzling in their own juices and the huge portion of shepherd's pie, McGuire's gave us a great time at an affordable price. Most impressive, however, is the ceiling, literally covered in dollar bills signed by decades' worth of inebriated fans. Each bill is stapled to the rafters, and we've got to guess

Dollar bills line the ceiling at McGuire's.

that the proprietor will retire someday on these tributes to his fine service. Open daily for lunch and dinner, with nightly drink specials. Sandwiches and traditional pub fare range from $9 to $17; entrees, $18 to $35.

The Native Café, 45 Via De Luna Drive, (850) 934-4848. The best breakfast on the beach is served here seven days a week, including simple choices like the three-egg-and-cheese omelet, eggs Benedict, pancakes stacked with local seasonal fruit, or the perfectly spiced, homemade apple-and-raisin oatmeal. Lunch (and dinner in summer) feature fresh ingredients, and not a single deep-fried anything—a real blessing in a seaside resort. What makes this diner special is the people you meet here, including proprietor Joyce Brown, who serves the tables personally and bakes up the most delicious desserts imaginable (be sure to ask about her scrumptious margarita cake). Open daily for breakfast and lunch, and dinner in the busy season; breakfast, $4–$8; lunch and dinner, $5–$10; plus some market-price items.

What to Do in Pensacola Beach

National Naval Aviation Museum, on Pensacola Naval Air Station, 1750 Radford Boulevard, Suite C, (800) 327-5002 or (850) 452-3604, www.naval aviationmuseum.org. With a collection of historic aircraft second only to the

The precision flying team The Blue Angels makes its home at Pensacola Naval Air Station.

Smithsonian, this museum will stir your heart with its combination of American innovation, military history, and stories of heroism. See what it feels like to fly an F-14 Tomcat fighter jet in the flight simulator, or walk through full-scale re-creations of an aircraft carrier, a 1940s Main Street, and an authentically detailed officers' club from World War II. An IMAX theater lets you experience flight on a seven-story screen. Museum admission is free. Open daily 9:00 a.m. to 5:00 p.m., closed Thanksgiving, Christmas, and New Year's Day.

Northwest Florida Zoo, 5701 Gulf Breeze Parkway, (850) 932-2229, www.thezoonorthwestflorida.org. Hippopotami, zebras, gorillas, lions, tigers, and 1,200 more animals are part of a collection of creatures from all over the world. The 30-acre preserve features an elevated boardwalk, giving you an upper-level view of the entire zoo, especially the free-ranging gorilla habitat—or take a train ride and get closer to the animals. You can even feed a giraffe by hand, or pet small animals in the Touch and Learn Farm. Admission is $8.25 for children three to eleven years old; $11.50 for adults ages twelve to sixty-one; and $10.50 for seniors sixty-two and over. Open daily from 9:00 a.m. to 5:00 p.m., closed Thanksgiving, Christmas Eve, and Christmas Day.

Ocean Springs: A Shining Recovery

While all eyes and cameras were on New Orleans during Hurricane Katrina in 2005, Ocean Springs, Mississippi, lay inundated to depths of 6 feet and more as the storm surge devastated the area. With the storms behind them and a new determination to revive their home city, local residents turned the town into a delightful village, with a meticulously preserved downtown historic area loaded with quirky shops, excellent restaurants, and a playful nightlife. Point your vehicle to the corner of Washington Avenue and Government Street, where you'll find a neighborhood with an upscale, stylish tone and plenty of inventive shopping and dining experiences.

Where to Stay in Ocean Springs

You'll find the popular hotel chains up at exit 50 off of I-10, but there are two accommodations closer to town that you won't want to miss.

Gulf Hills Hotel & Conference Center, 13701 Paso Road, (228) 875-4211, www.gulfhillshotel.com. Renovated in 2002–03, this historic hotel and conference center was once the inn of choice for a famous native Mississippian: Elvis Presley. Today, you can stay in the Elvis Suite, a truly extraordinary set of rooms with the 6-foot-high bed headboards you might see at Graceland, and plenty of authentic memorabilia from the star's career. Conventional suites and standard rooms, complimentary deluxe continental breakfast, an on-site grill and lounge, a pool and tennis courts, and use of the golf course across the front lawn make this a relaxed, easy place

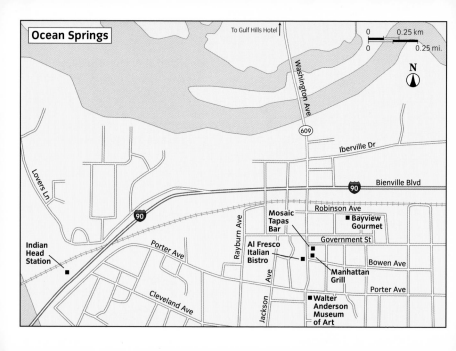

Ocean Springs

To Gulf Hills Hotel

Washington Ave

609

0   0.25 km
0   0.25 mi.

N

Iberville Dr

90   Bienville Blvd

Robinson Ave

Rayburn Ave

Mosaic
Tapas
Bar

Bayview
Gourmet

Government St

90

Al Fresco
Italian
Bistro

Manhattan
Grill

Bowen Ave

Indian
Head
Station

Porter Ave

Jackson Ave

Porter Ave

Lovers Ln

Cleveland Ave

Walter
Anderson
Museum
of Art

to spend a few days. Standard rooms range from $109 to $129; suites, $300 to $500; Elvis Suite, 700 to $1,000.

Indian Head Station, 500 Bienville Boulevard, (228) 818-1801, www .indianheadstation.com. The creation of its visionary owner, Melanie Bosarge, this bed-and-breakfast style inn was a Super 8 until 2005, when storm waters forced its closing. Seeing its potential, Bosarge stepped in and turned it into a sweet boutique hotel. Each room bears evidence of the owner's Delta charm, with travertine counters, crown molding, wrought-iron fixtures and trim, and real china bowls and coffee mugs; even the towels have embroidered designs and appliqués. Hanging flower baskets planted by hand, a carefully landscaped garden

with tropical plants, and spaces for fishermen to park their boats and sleep inside in comfort all make this hotel a special place. Rooms are $79 to $129; call for rates for extended stays.

Where to Eat in Ocean Springs

For dining with a creative flair, try one of these intriguing experiences—but note that all of the downtown restaurants are closed on Sunday.

Al Fresco Italian Bistro, 708 Washington Avenue, (228) 818-9395, www .alfrescoitalianbistro.com. You didn't expect to find veal osso bucco or stuffed cannelloni in Mississippi? Neither did we, but this Tuscan-style bistro crosses Italian favorites with Cajun,

Thai, and French flavors to create a menu that's innovative and delicious. Try the crawfish etouffee penne, or the shrimp and duck fettuccini for a different kind of adventure in taste. Lunch and dinner, Monday through Saturday, $13 to $34.

Bayview Gourmet Restaurant, 1010 Robinson Avenue, (228) 875-4252, www.bayviewgourmet.com. Sunday brunch here is a must, with every conceivable combination of eggs, pancakes, waffles, hash browns or grits, and breakfast meats. Try the sweet potato pancakes, or sample Cajun grilled tomatoes as a side dish. Open Tuesday through Sunday, breakfast and lunch only. Breakfast $7.00–$11.50, lunch $8.25–$13.00.

Manhattan Grill, 705 Washington Avenue, (228) 872-6480. Fine dining at its best lives in this sophisticated steak house, where entrees range from grilled duck breast with red wine sauce and portabella mushrooms to filet mignon topped with lump crabmeat, and nightly specials demonstrate the chef's creativity with fresh local foods. Reservations are strongly recommended, especially on weekends. Open Monday through Saturday for lunch and dinner, $25–$35.

Mosaic Tapas Bar, 1010 Government Street, (228) 818-9885. Choose several little plates from a selection of more than twenty, from ceviche del mar—local red snapper with citrus juice, serrano pepper, and cilantro—

to crab cakes, grilled fish tacos, pork marinated in achiote and served with habanero sauce, or calamari romano. Your meal is served in an intimate dining room where nightly live music can range from Brazilian jazz to Mississippi blues. Mosaic offers a hookah bar as well, an unusual experience in fragrance and taste involving very little tobacco. Open for lunch and dinner, Tuesday through Saturday. Each plate is $3.50–$10.00.

What to Do in Ocean Springs

Walter Anderson Museum of Art, 500 Washington Avenue, (228) 872-3164, www.walterandersonmuseum.org. The work of Anderson, famous for his watercolors and drawings of Davis Bayou and other areas in and around Ocean Springs, is showcased here alongside regional art by his relatives, Peter and Mac Anderson. Open Monday through Saturday, 9:30 a.m. to 4:30 p.m., and Sunday 12:30 to 4:30 p.m. Adults $7, seniors $6, and $5 for children between five and fifteen years old.

Shop. Sample praline logs at the Candy Cottage, find unusual gifts at Art & Soul, discover women's fashions at The Bay Collection or Bayou Belle, or find ceramics by local artists at Fort Bayou Pottery & Gifts. The Washington Avenue / Government Street area offers these boutiques and many more, providing you with unusual gift ideas well beyond the ordinary.

Resources

Ocean Springs Chamber of Commerce, 1000 Washington Avenue, Ocean Springs, (228) 875-4424, www.ocean springschamber.com

Pensacola Beach Chamber of Commerce, 735 Pensacola Beach Boulevard, (850) 932-1500, www.visitpensacola beach.com

Santa Rosa Island Authority, 1 Via De Luna Drive, Pensacola Beach, (850) 932-2257, sria-fla.com

Vacation Rental Services

Emerald Coast Rentals, (850) 343-2255, (866) 884-7419, www.pensacola beach-rentals.com

Pensacola Beach House Rental, www .beachhouse.com/travelogue/Pensacola-Beach-House-Rental.htm

Pensacola Beach Vacation Guide, www.pensacolabeach.com

Fishing Charters

Pensacola Beach:

Beach Marina Fishing Fleet and Sunset Cruises, 655 Pensacola Beach Boulevard, (850) 932-0304, www .pensacolabeachmarina.com

Pensacola Beach Gulf Pier, 41 Fort Pickens Road, (850) 934-7200, www .fishpensacolabeachpier.com

Ocean Springs/Biloxi:

Chandeleur Outfitters, LLC, 1106 Government Street, Ocean Springs, (228) 818-0030, www.chandeleuroutfitters.com

Strictly Fishin' Charters, Harbor Landing Slip #1, 1709 Harbor Road, Ocean Springs, (228) 217-0458, www.strictly fishincharters.com

Index

Copyright © 2009 Morris Book Publishing, LLC

All photos © Nic Minetor.
Text design by Mary Ballachino
Maps created by XNR Productions, Inc. © Morris Book Publishing, LLC
Many thanks to Gail Bishop, chief of interpretation at Gulf Islands National Seashore, as well as chief ranger Clayton Jordan; ranger-interpreters Mike Aymond, David Ogden, and Stacy Speas; Mississippi District interpretive supervisor Susan Blair; fee manager Sally Lewis; national seashore volunteers Rick Keller and Sigrid Benson; and Hal Harris of Fort Pickens Shuttle Service, for their invaluable insights and assistance. Very special thanks to Eric Fundin and the production staff at WSRE-TV in Pensacola, Florida, for their partnership in this project.

Library of Congress Cataloging-in-Publication Data is available.
ISBN 978-0-7627-5309-3

Printed in China
10 9 8 7 6 5 4 3 2 1

The prices, rates, and hours of operation listed in this guidebook were confirmed at press time. We recommend, however, that you call establishments before traveling to obtain current information.